Beautiful Nude Women from the Orient

A Journey through colonial Northern Africa

Jürgen Prommersberger: A Journey through Colonial Northern Africa
Regenstauf , January 2016

All rights reserved:
Jürgen Prommersberger
Händelstr 17
93128 Regenstauf

First edition by
CreateSpace Independent Publishing Platform

Foreword

Slavery and "honor" in Islamic societies

Slaves had in Islamic societies officially no honor. The status as a slave meant, that they lived a separate life, which was different from the life and status of normal people in regard of kinship, family and religion. Once in enslavement, social norms, resulting from kinship or religion, were completely ignored. Slaves were exempted from all social rights, including the right over their own bodies and their own sexuality, but they were also exempted from obligations, constraints and responsibilities, which were part of the lives of the free individuals in the social community. This was particularly important for the social value "honor". Every free individual possessed honor, no matter if man or woman.

The existence of a term as "honor" therefore means, that there must be something on the opposite side like "shame". A shame arises always from the violation of a universal, social norm. It is less important to know whether this standard is codified as law or whether it is a social standard. As a slave, a man or a woman had officially no honor, therefore there was also nothing for which a slave would or could be ashamed of. Where there is no honor, there is also no shame.

A free Muslim woman was breaking these social rules of honor, if she left the house without her body being completely covered. If you look nowadays to Saudi Arabia, to Iran and also to other countries in the arab world, then you have to realize, that this „Law" is still in force and a woman can get into trouble, when she goes out without the so-called Burka (a clothing, which is covering a woman from the head to the toes completely). On the other hand, female slaves could go out as light clothed as they liked, because nudity in public was no official offence for a person who had no honour at all.

This illustrated book shows such women. Slaves, dancers, prostitutes, masseuses. All girls and women, who possessed in the eyes of the „normal" society no honor and had therefore no need to be ashamed of their nakedness, no matter if only topless or completely nude.

These photos were taken mostly from the former colonial territories of France. So mainly from Morocco, Algeria and Tunisia. The pictures date back tot he late 19th century until around the times of the first world war.

JEUNE BARBARINE

Types du MAROC. - Esclave

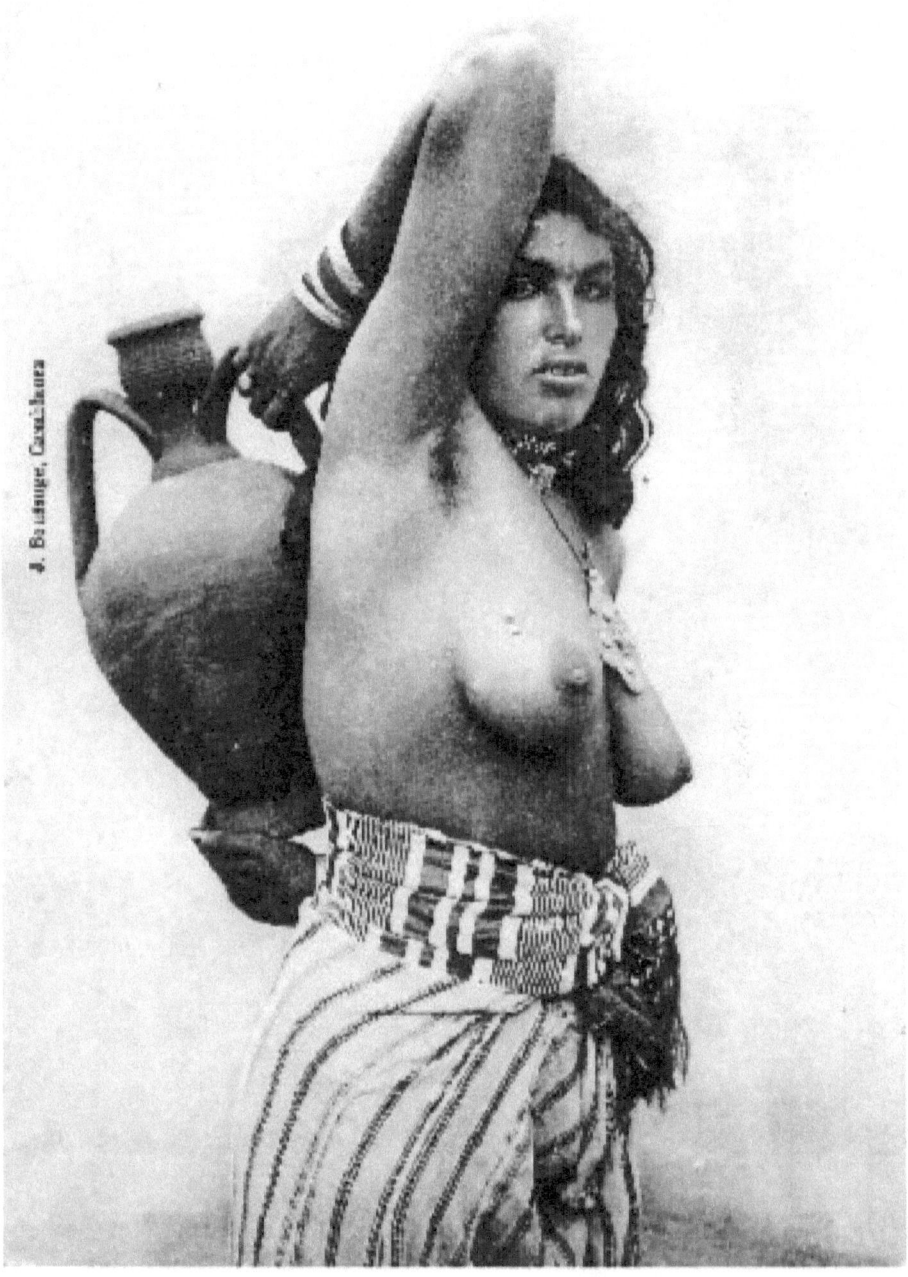

BÉDOUINE REVENANT DE LA CITERNE

TANGER
Joven Marroquí

843 A　　　　Mauresque.　　　　P. Cousin et Cie, Rabat

73. - MAROC. - Une Femme à Fez

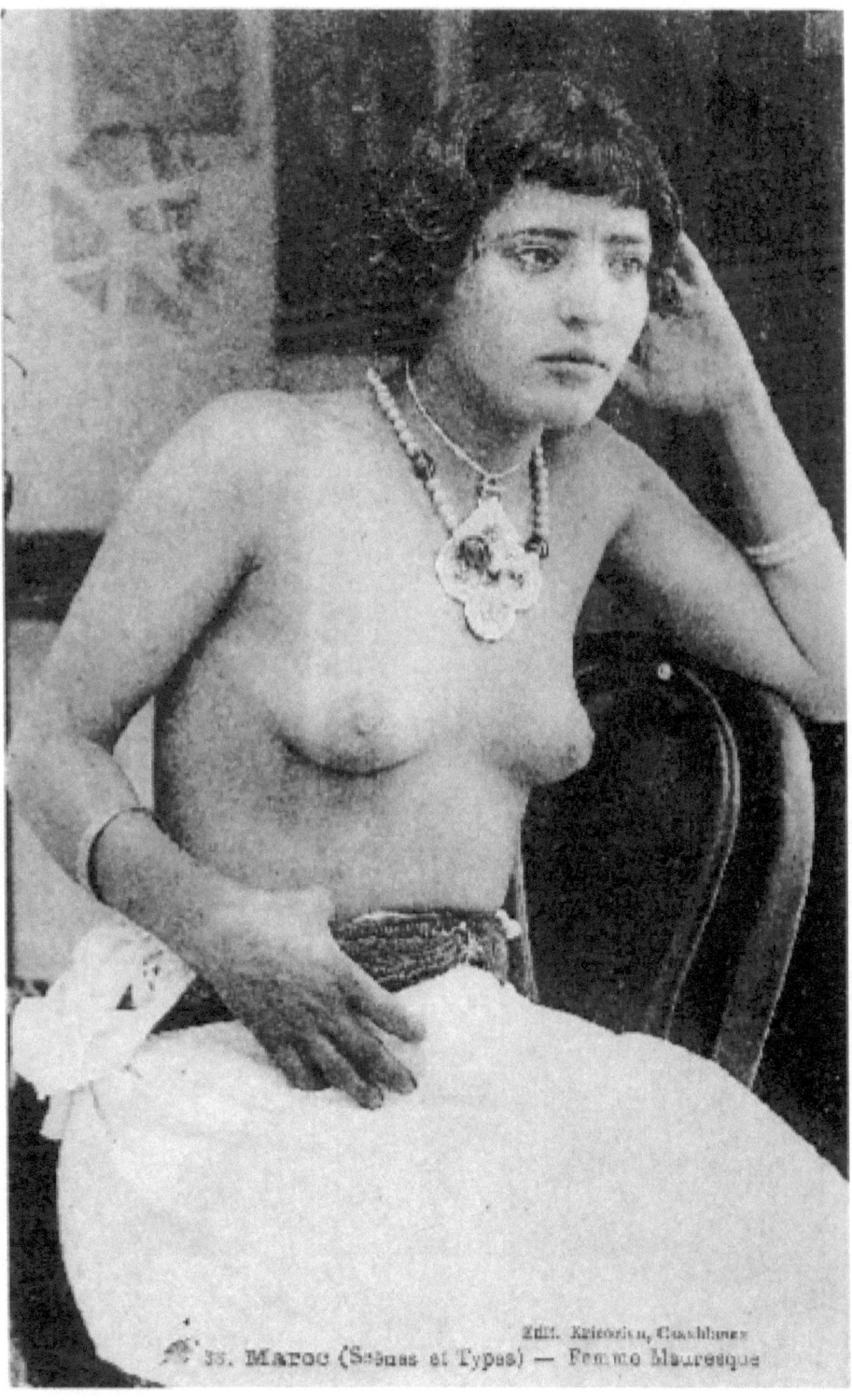

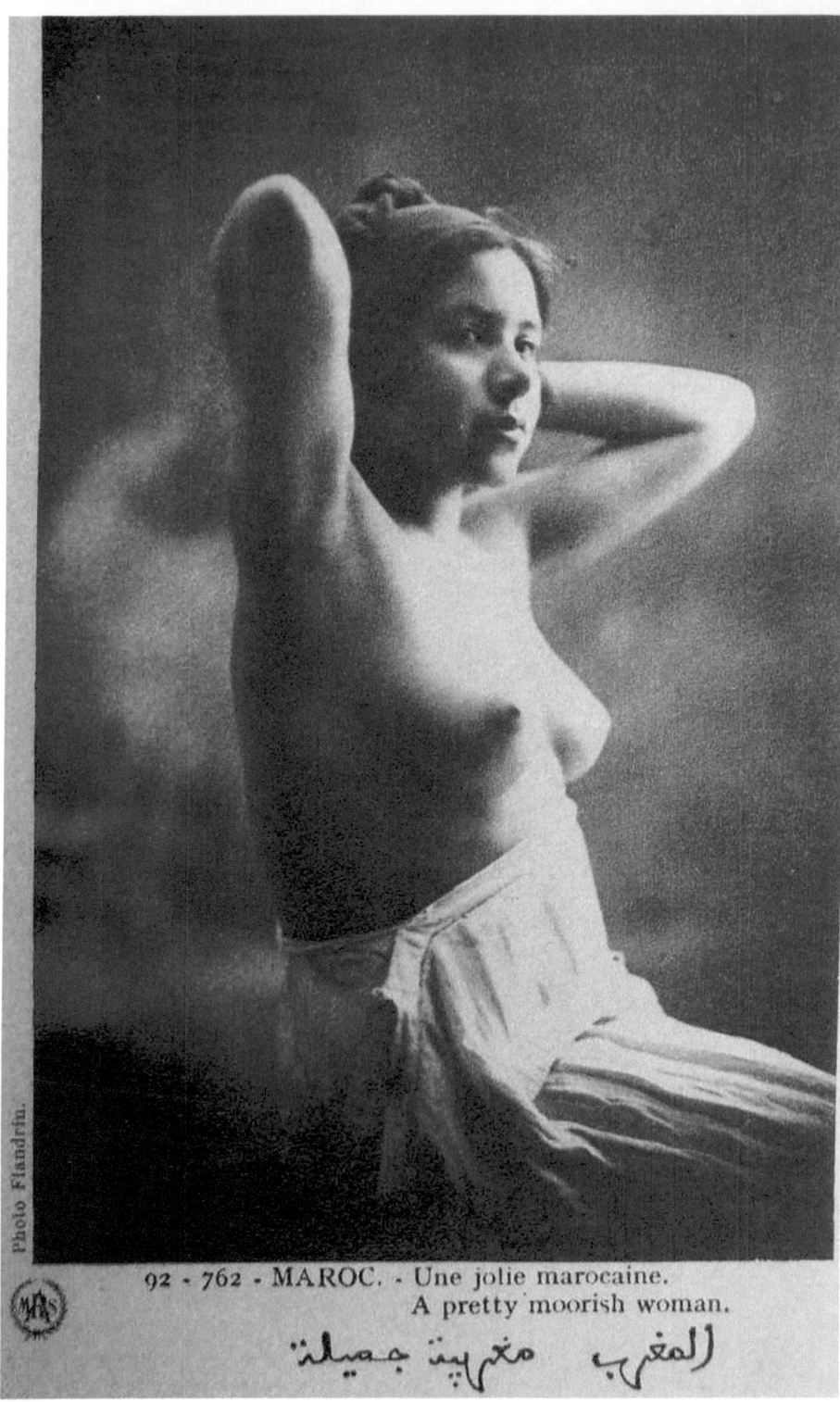

92 - 762 - MAROC. - Une jolie marocaine.
A pretty moorish woman.

SOUVENIR D'ORIENT
Danse Orientale

Photo Flandrin · 797. - MAROC. — La favorite après le bain.

606. — ESCLAVES DANS LES BANANIERS.

Photo Flandrin 713. MAROC — Le Sourire de Yamina !

Photo Flandria 712. MAROC
Au Quartier réservé - Une femme du Sud

Photo Flandrin 681. MAROC — La danse du ventre

Photo Flandrin 680. Femme Marocaine

16. — Esclaves sur la terrasse d'une casbah féodale.

614. — ESCLAVE A LA FONTAINE.

Photo Flandrin 589. - MAROC — Jeune berbère nue.

61 - MAROC - Fleur de brousse
Photo Flandrin Reprod. Interd.

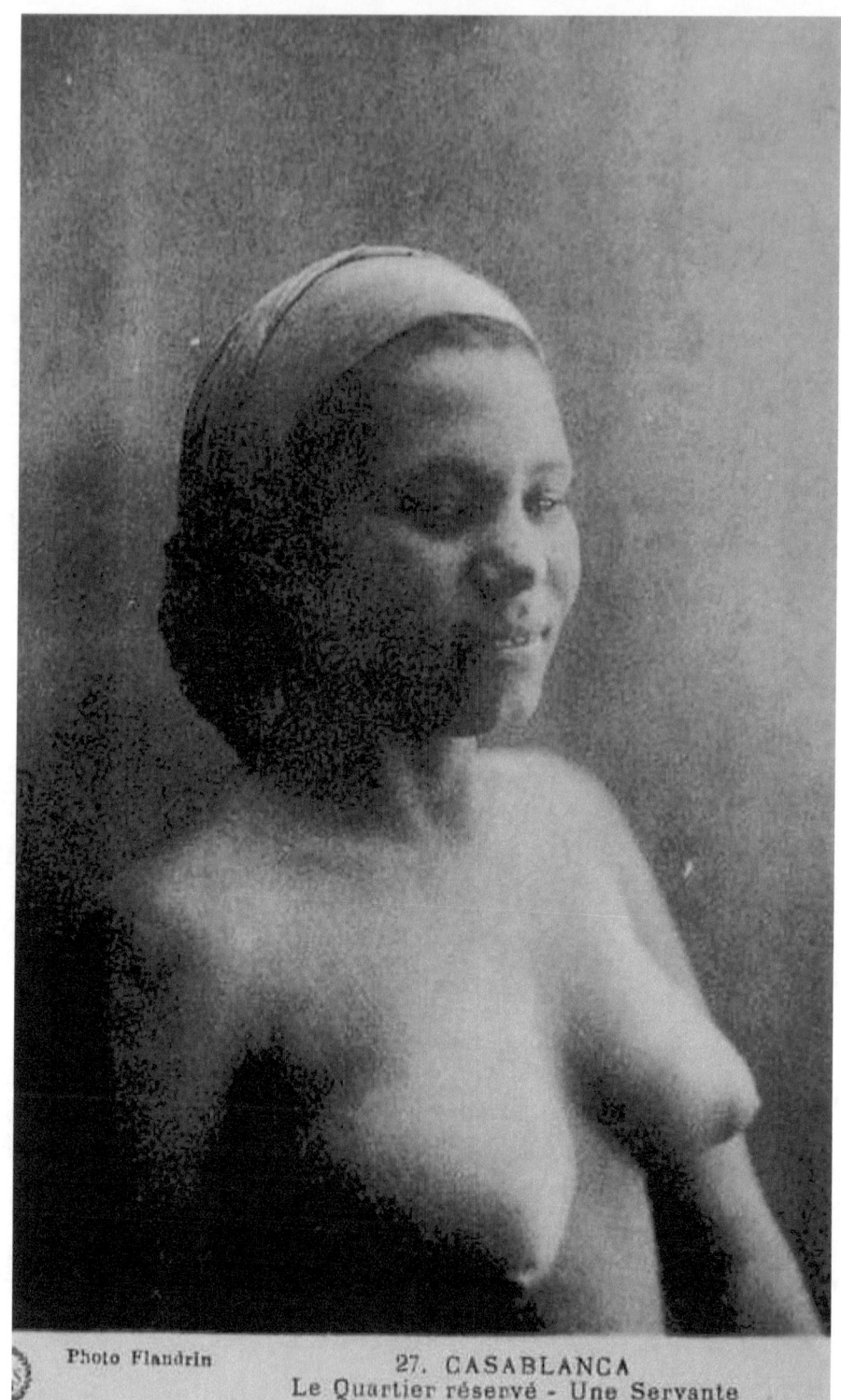

Photo Flandrin — 27. CASABLANCA
Le Quartier réservé - Une Servante

Photo Flandrin 26. CASABLANCA
Au Quartier réservé - Une hétaïre de luxe

23. CASABLANCA — Le quartier réservé - Une tangéroise
Photo Flandrin

Photo Flandrin 20. CASABLANCA
Le Quartier réservé - Une jolie Mauresque

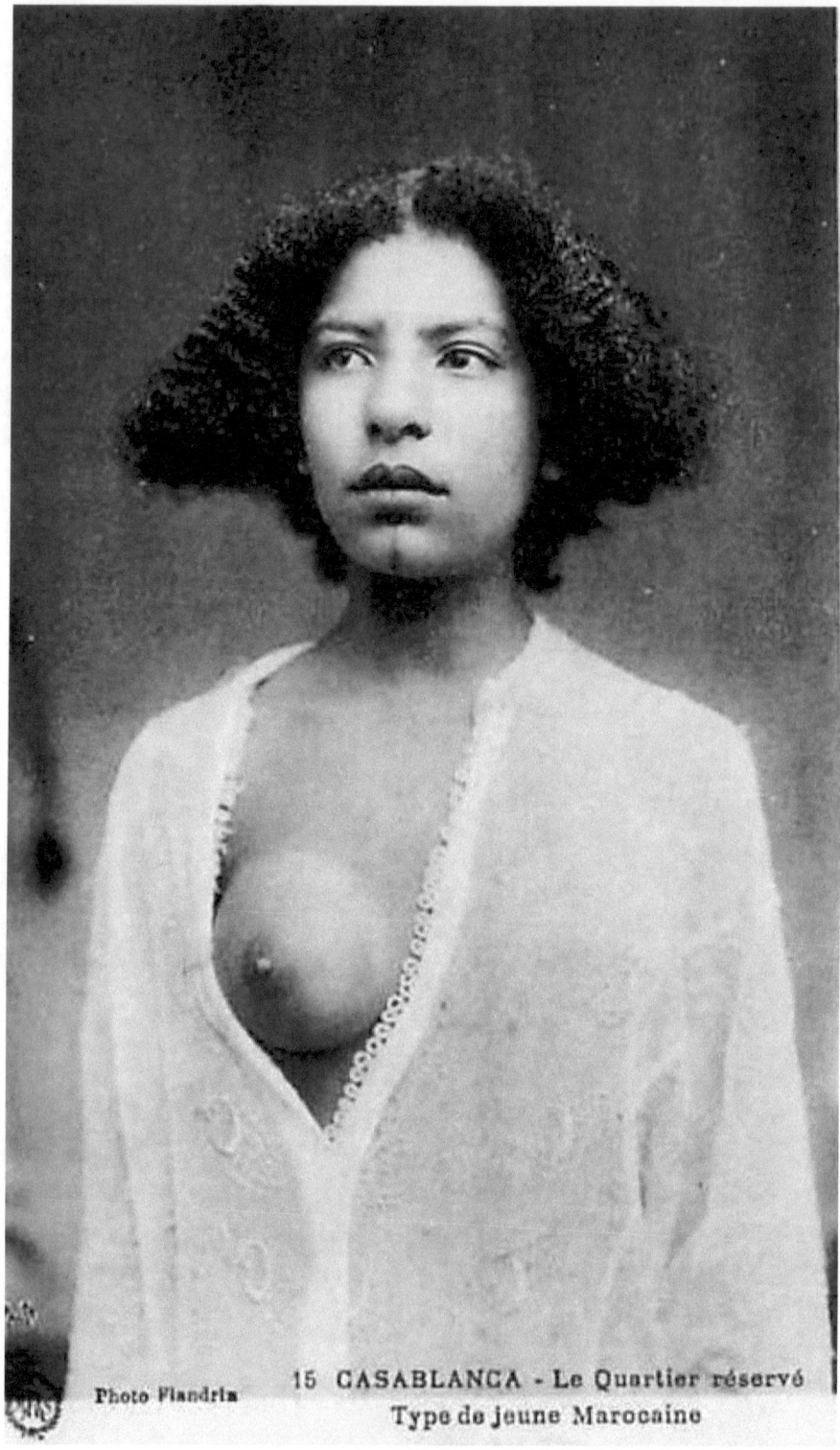

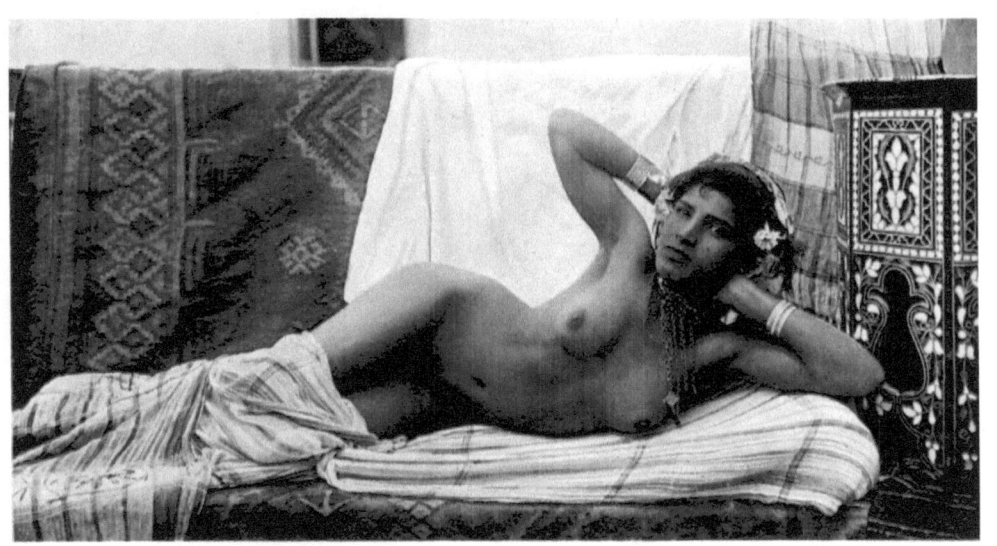

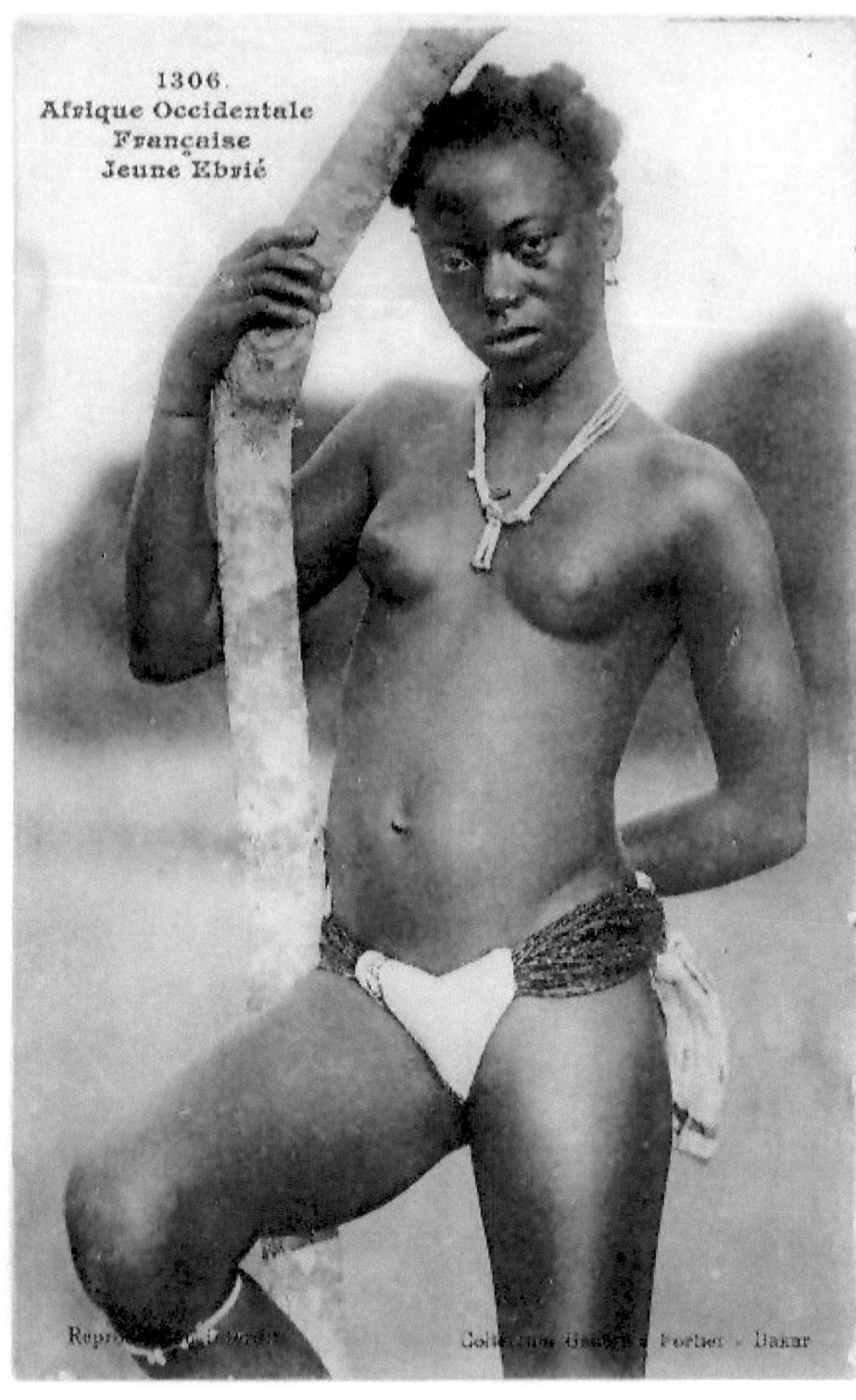

1065. Afrique Occidentale - SÉNÉGAL — Femme "Ouolof"

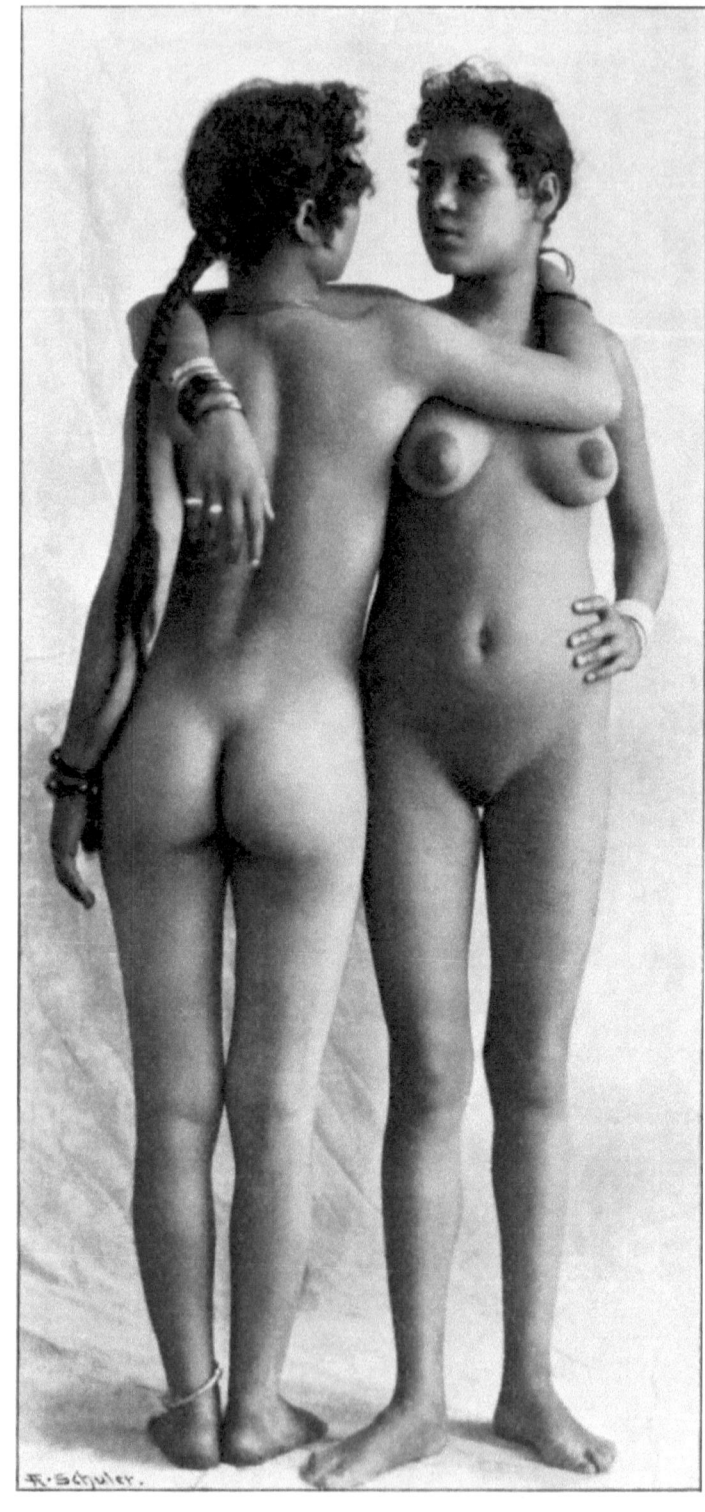

853 Fillette arabe

711 - Les deux amies.

538 - Jeune femme arabe.

133 T Mauresques.

631 Une Almée

J. Geiser, phot.-Alger.

585 Masseuse de bain maure

J. Geiser, phot.-Alger

582 Bédouines dans leur intérieur

450 ALGÉRIE. — Mauresque dans son intérieur

528 Jeune fille du Sud

J. Geiser, phot.-Alger.

faudrais de te voir avant
de quitter Zaza j'ai vu le
d'lieutenant de l'aviation
un bon copain. et comme
tu m'avais
dit que
tu voulais si tu
venir au y tiens
Maroc_ je te
et je mettrai
crois qu'il en relation
pourrait avec lui.
te faire
venir en Je t'em
remontant brasse
avec un cinq
type cent fois
 Marly

523 Jeune mauresque

J. Geiser, phot. — Alger.

487 Une almée

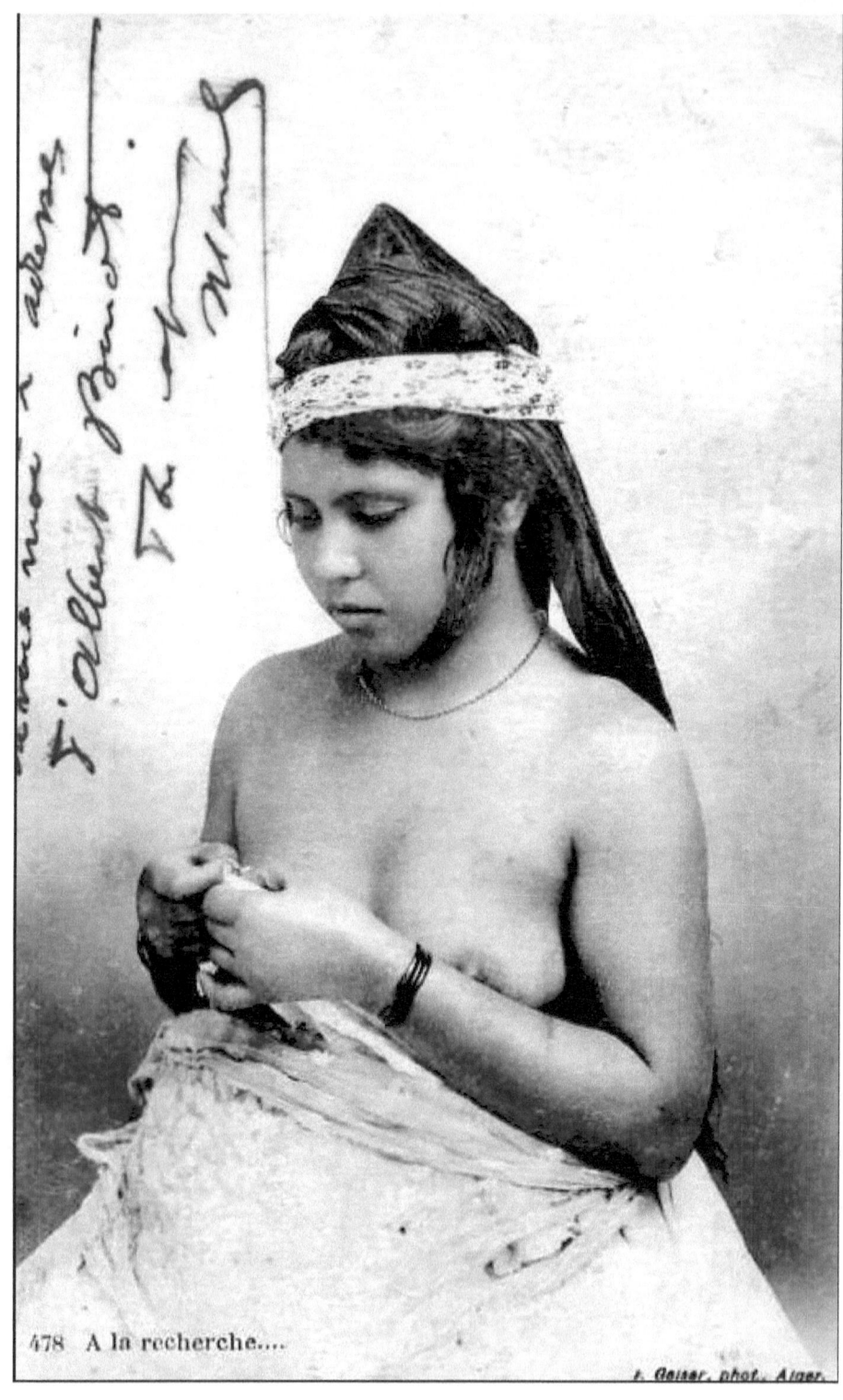

478 A la recherche....

475 Bédouine tunisienne

J. Geiser, phot.-Alger

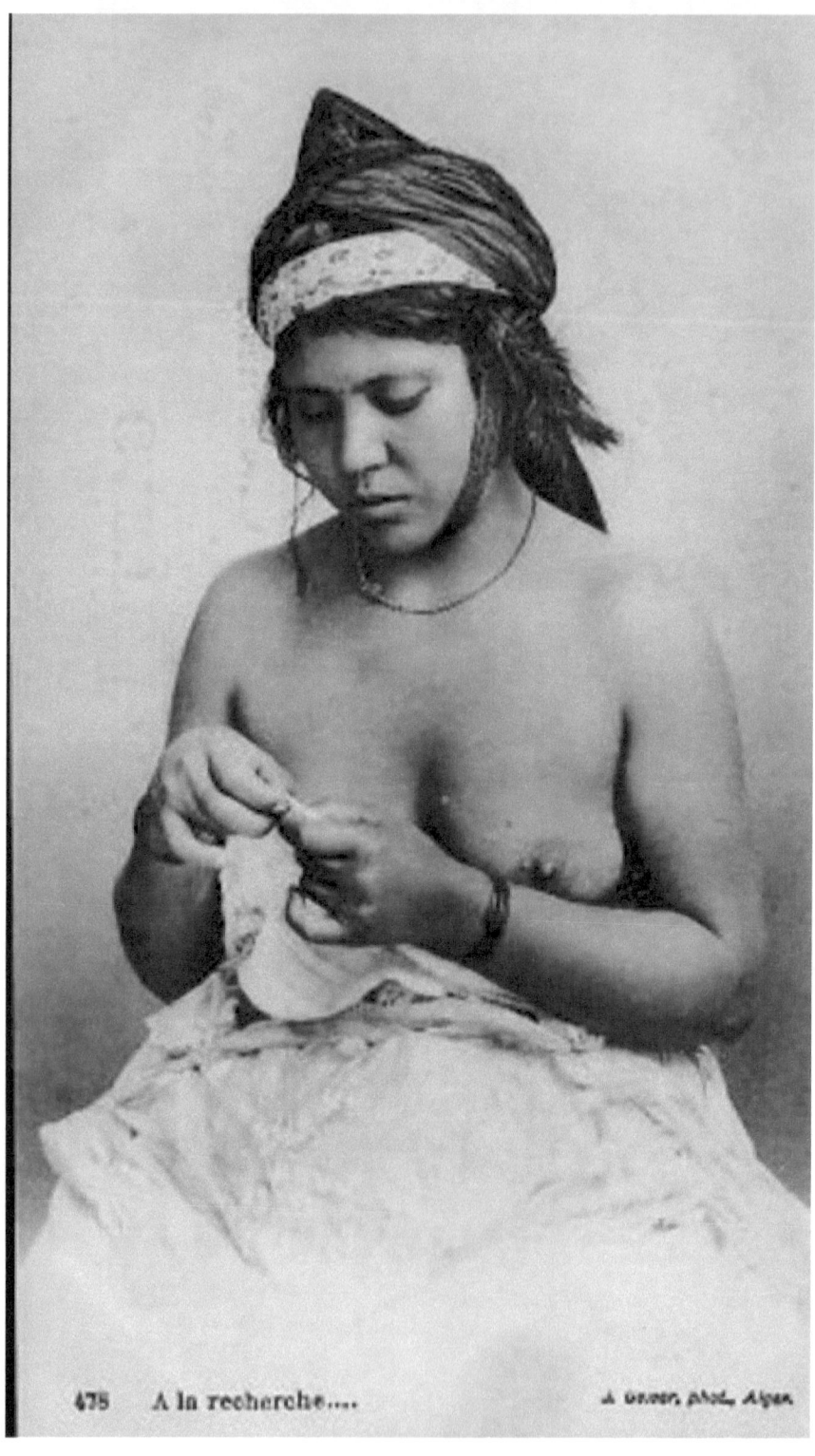

475 A la recherche.... A. Geiser, phot., Alger

441 ALGÉRIE. — Masseuse de bain maure
J. GEISER, ALGER.

437 ALGERIE. — Femme de l'Extrême-Sud
J. Geiser, phot. — Alger.

431 Mauresque dans son intérieur J. Geiser, phot. — Alger

374 Mauresque dans son intérieur J. Geiser, phot.-Alger

423 Danse du tambourin

421 La danse du sabre

J. Geiser, phot.-Alger

417 Jeune fille du Sud

Algérie. — *Masseuse de Bain maure*

La danse

Algérie. — *Danse du ventre*

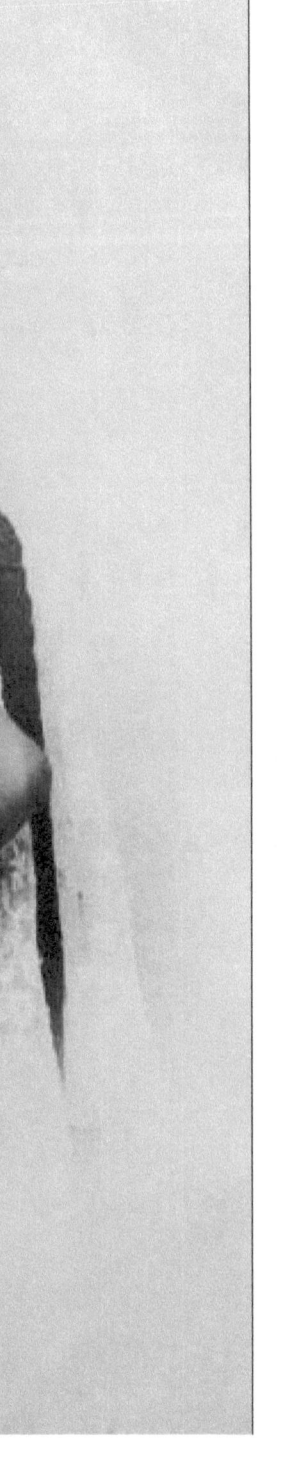

273 Jeune mauresque

J. Geiser, Alger

272 Femme du Sud

J. Geiser, phot.-Alger.

271 Mauresque danseuse
J. Geiser-Alger

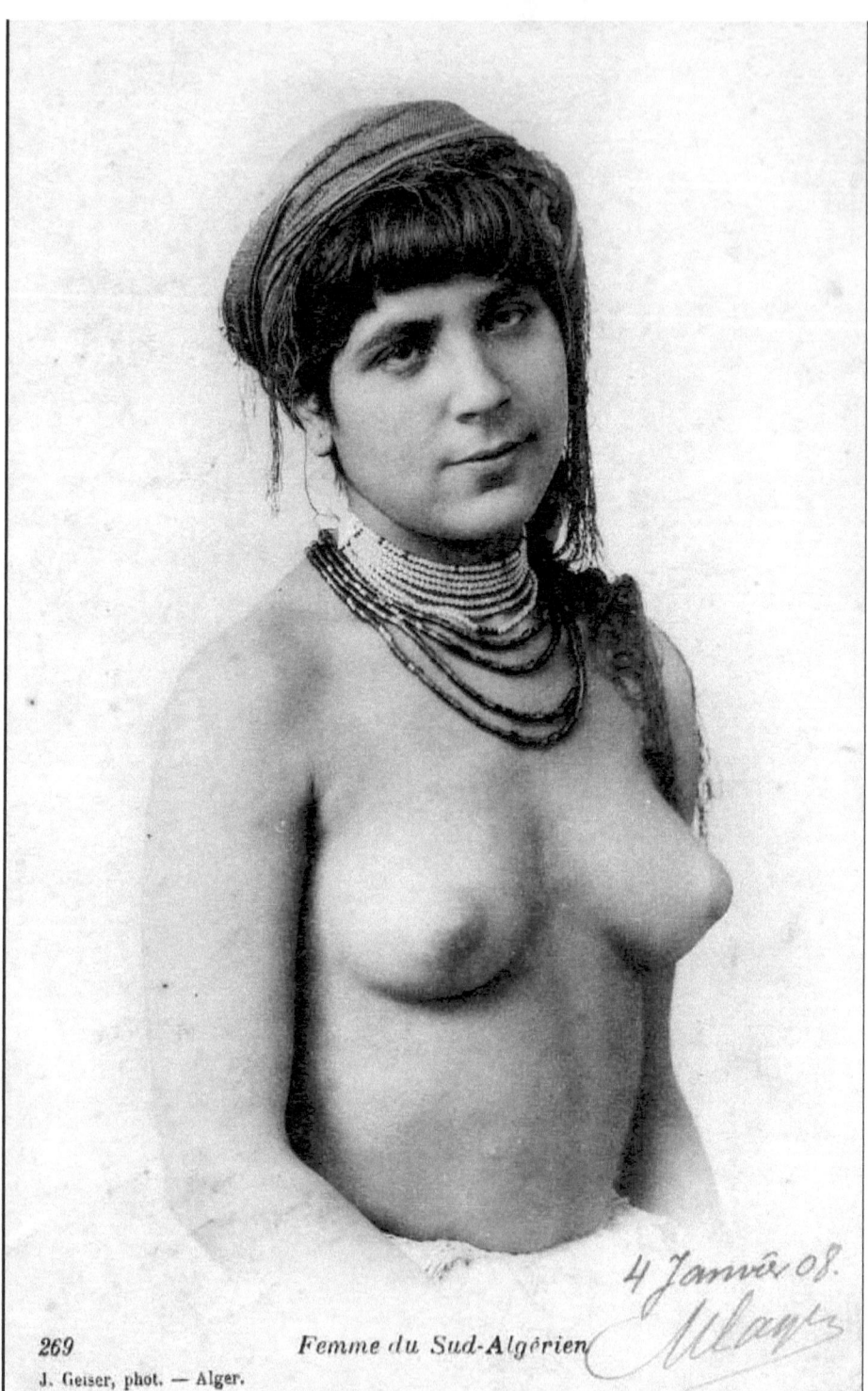

Bédouine

J. Geiser, Alger

Femme du Sud-Algérien

Femme du Sud-Algérien

La danse du ventre

Jeune Bédouine

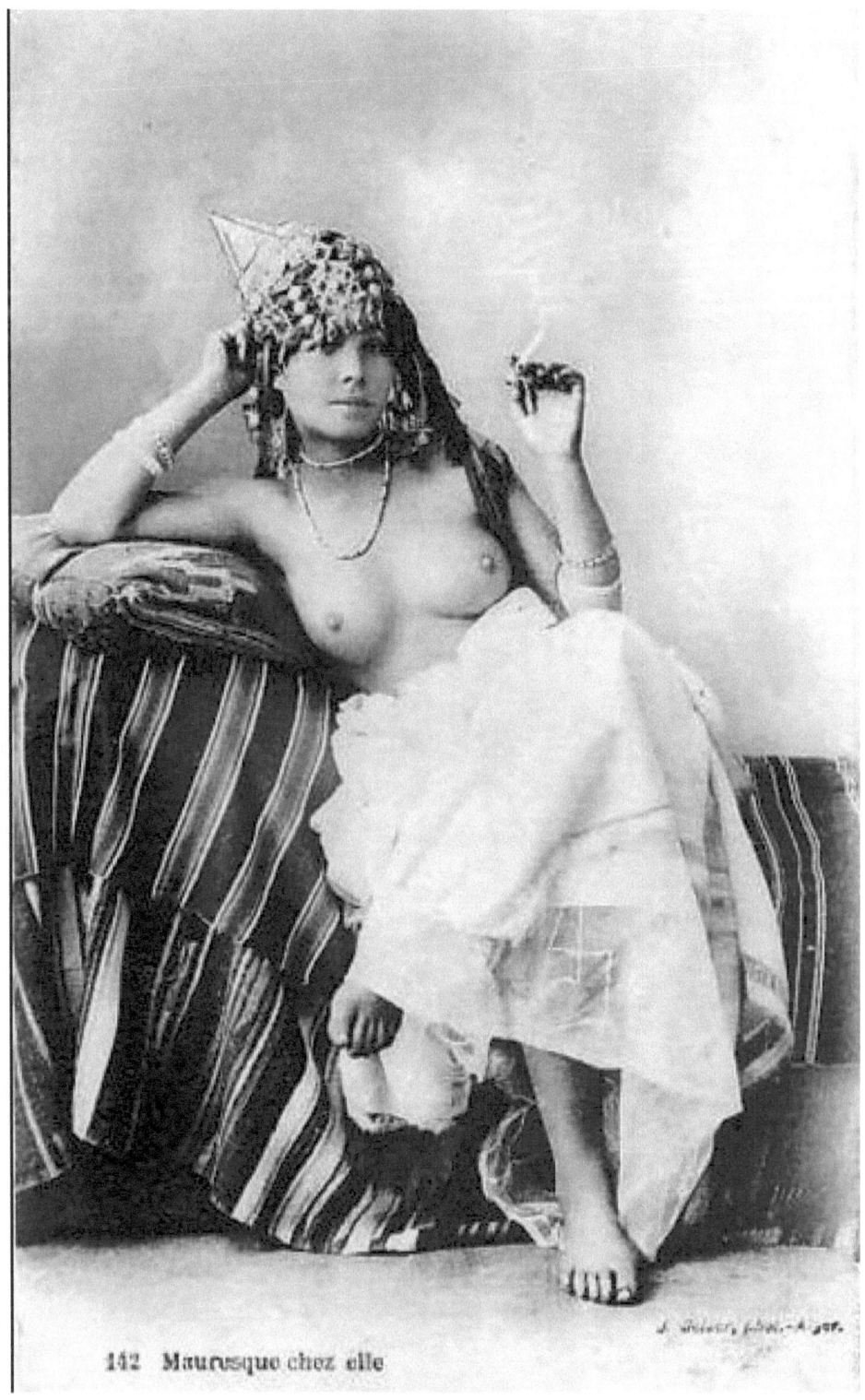

142 Mauresque chez elle

Femme du Sud Algérien. — La danse

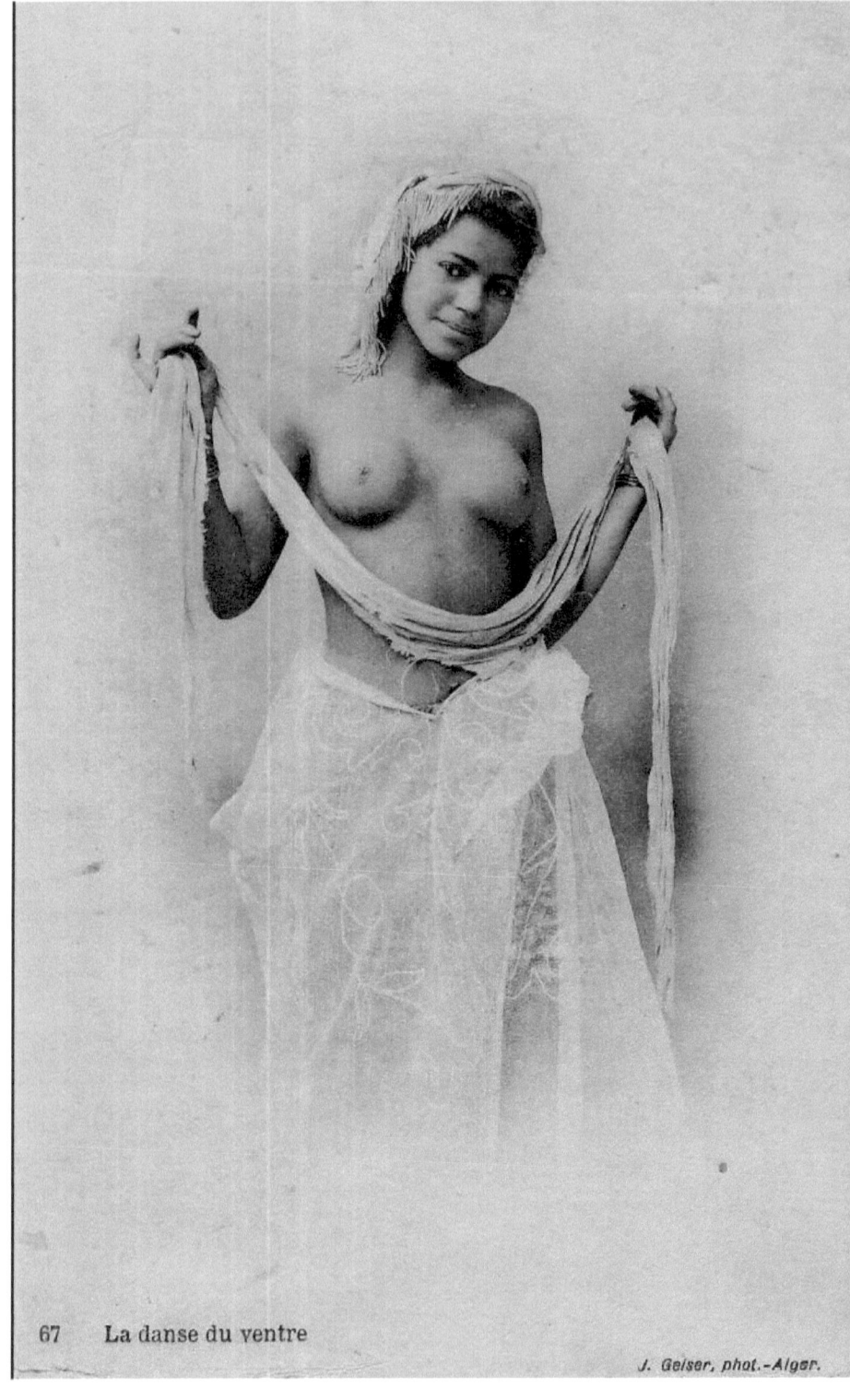

67 La danse du ventre

J. Geiser, phot.-Alger.

Une almée

ALGÉRIE. — Femme du Sud

31 Jolie danseuse

30 - Jeune Bédouine

1142. AFRIQUE du NORD — Femme berbère

227 La danse du ventre

J. Geiser, phot., Alger.

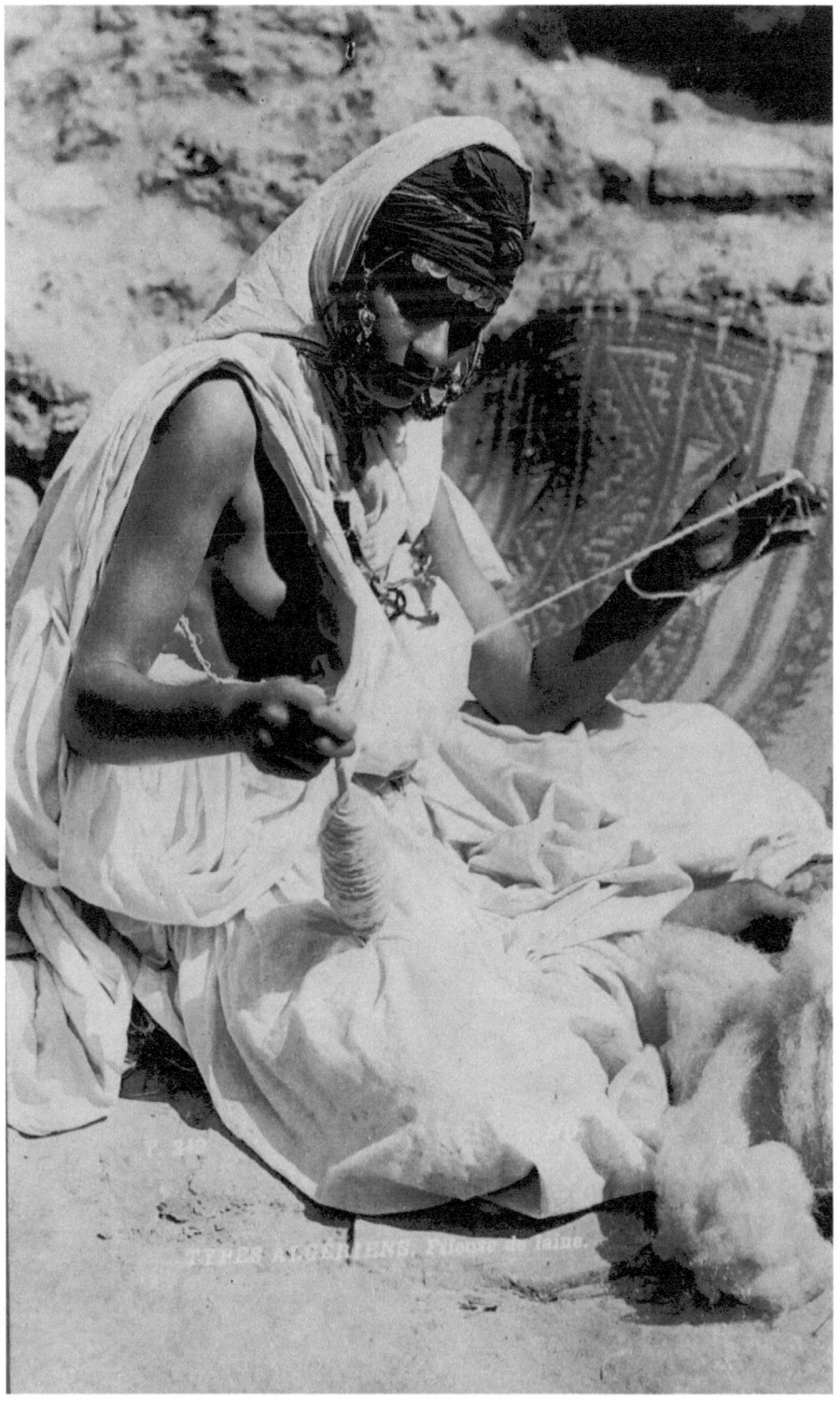

872 A *Jeune Femme kabyle parée de ses bijoux*

876 A Jeune Femme Kabyle parée de ses bijoux. ND. Phot.

866. SCÈNES ET TYPES. Jeune Femme Kabyle parée de ses bijoux. ND

821 A — Mauresques. — Collection Spéciale P. A. — ND. Phot.

862 A — Jeune Femme kabyle parée de ses bijoux.
Collection spéciale P. A.

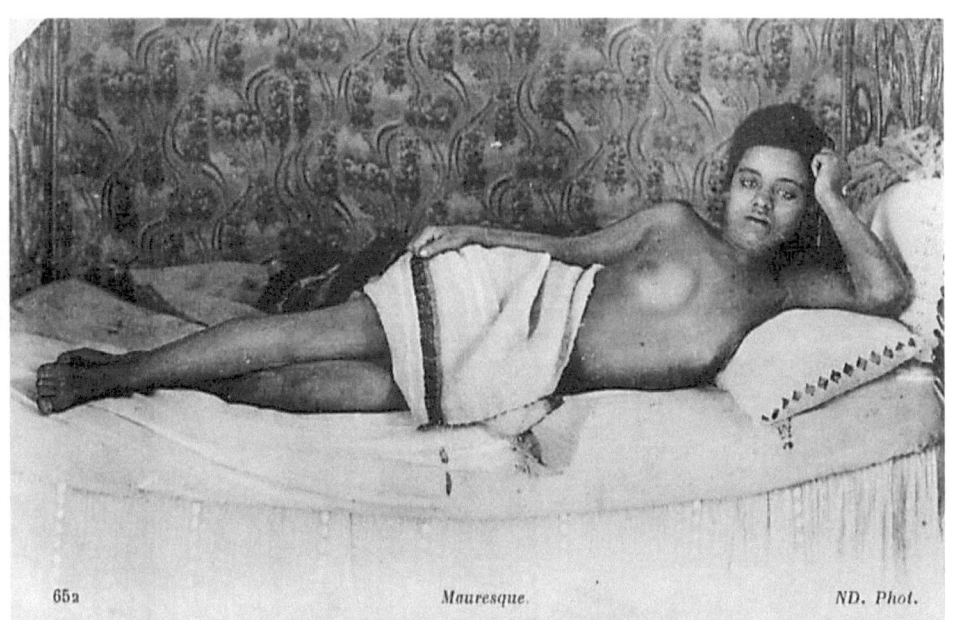

652 *Mauresque.* ND. Phot.

583 A — *Mauresque.* ND. Phot.

606 T — JEUNES BÉDOUINES — ND

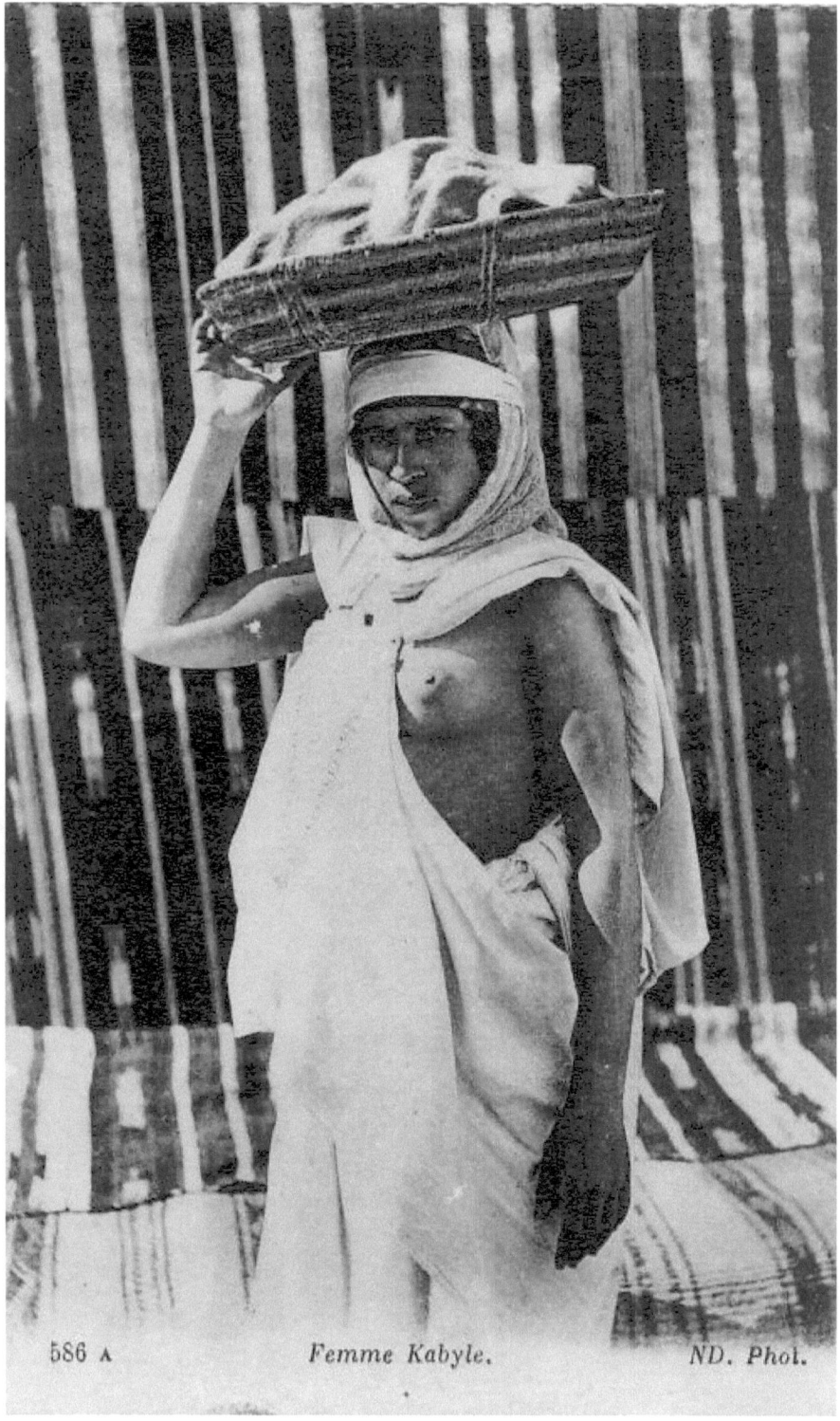

586 A — Femme Kabyle. — ND. Phot.

581 a Mauresque. — ND Phot.

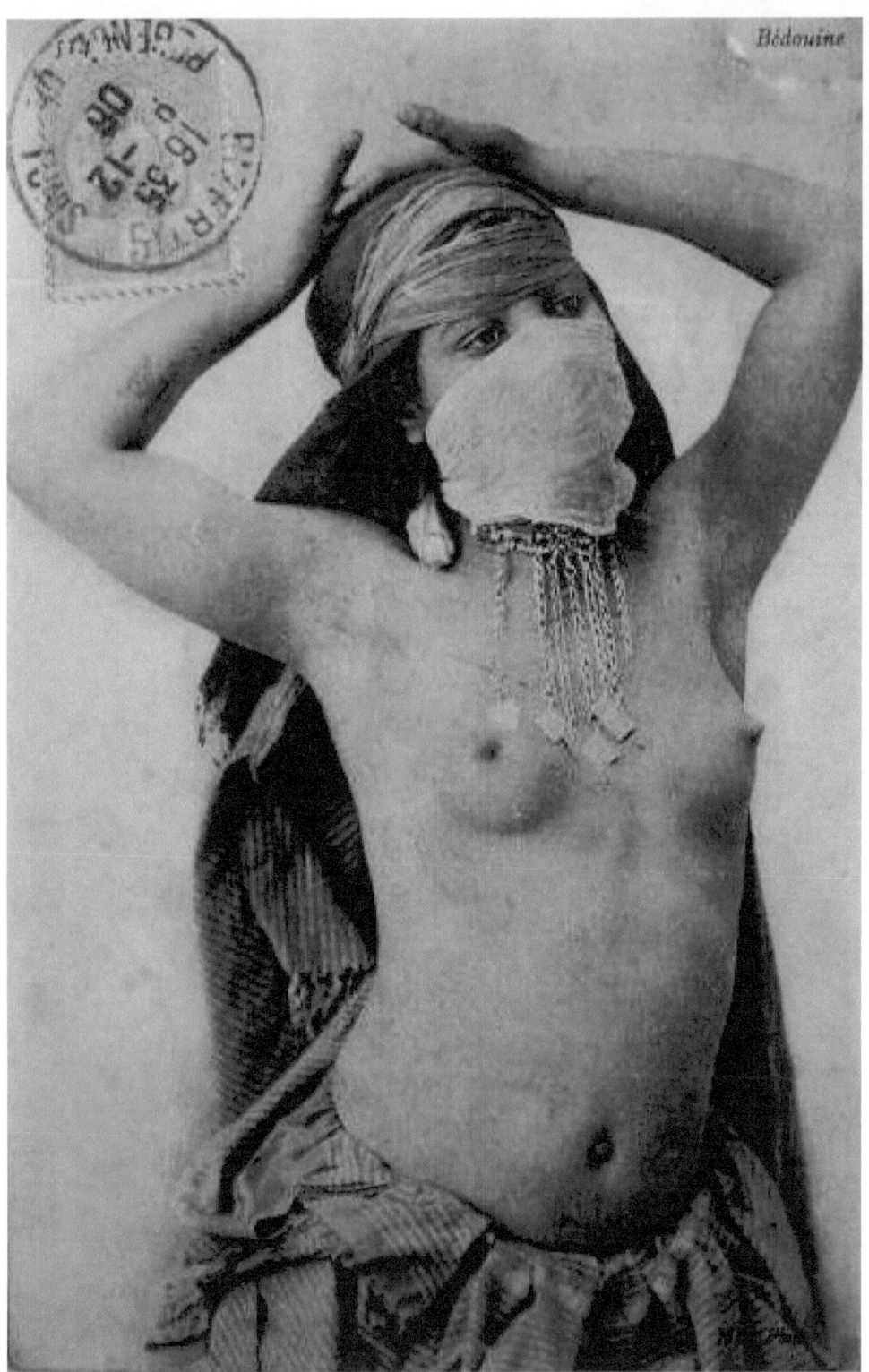

Chanteuse Arabe.

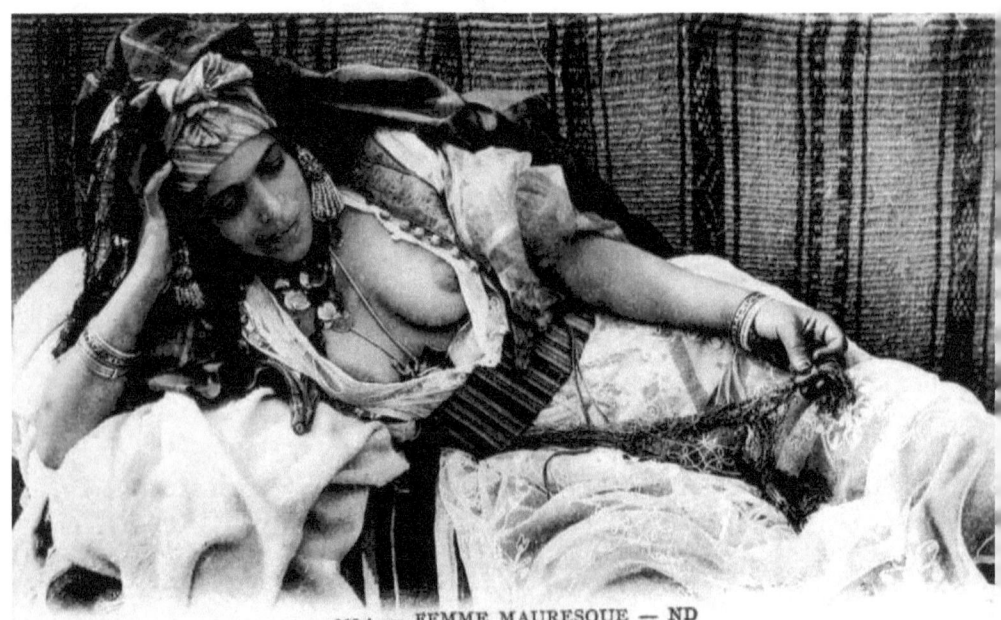

Jeune Mauresque et Femme Kabyle. ND, Phot.

229 A — FEMME MAURESQUE — ND

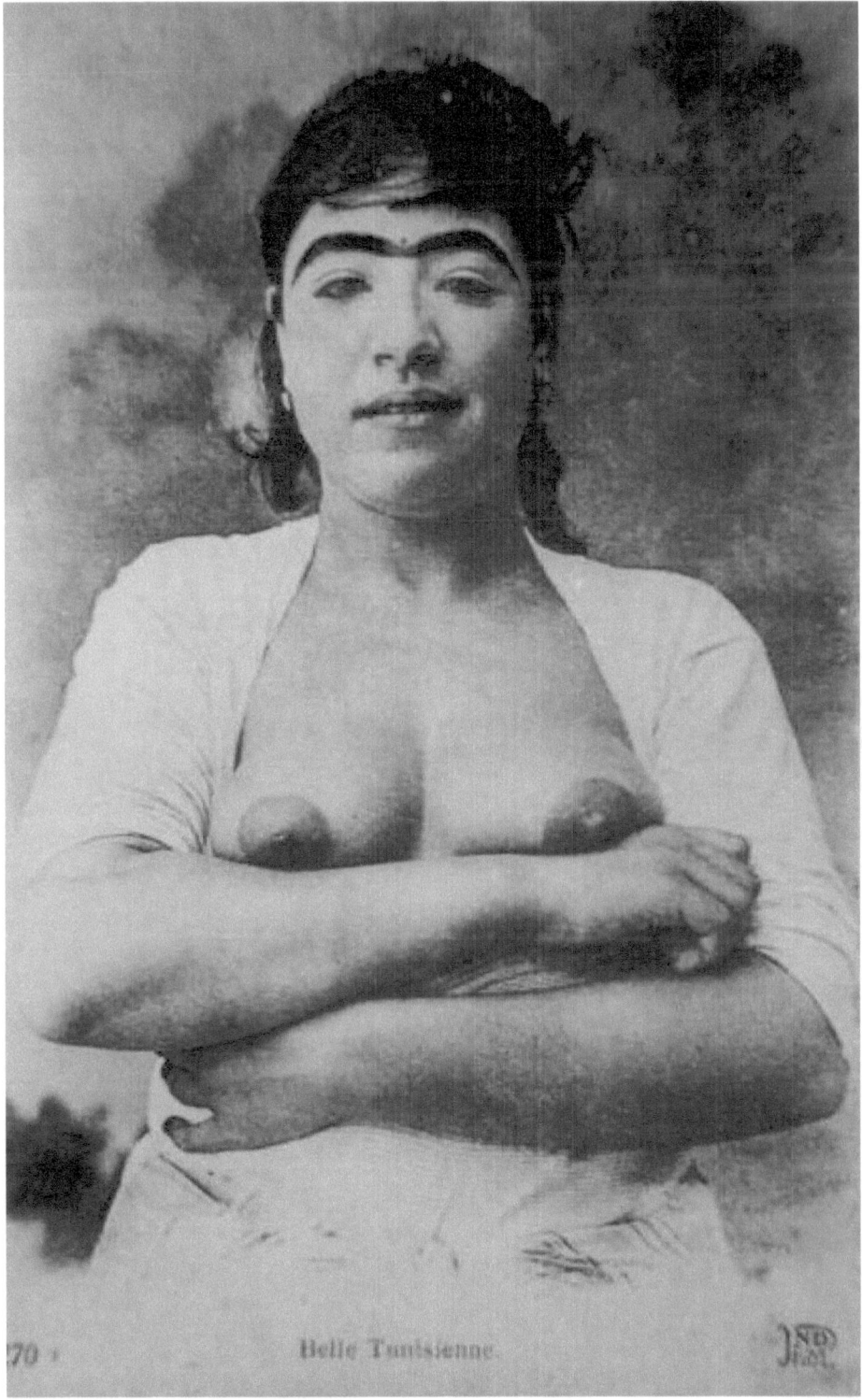

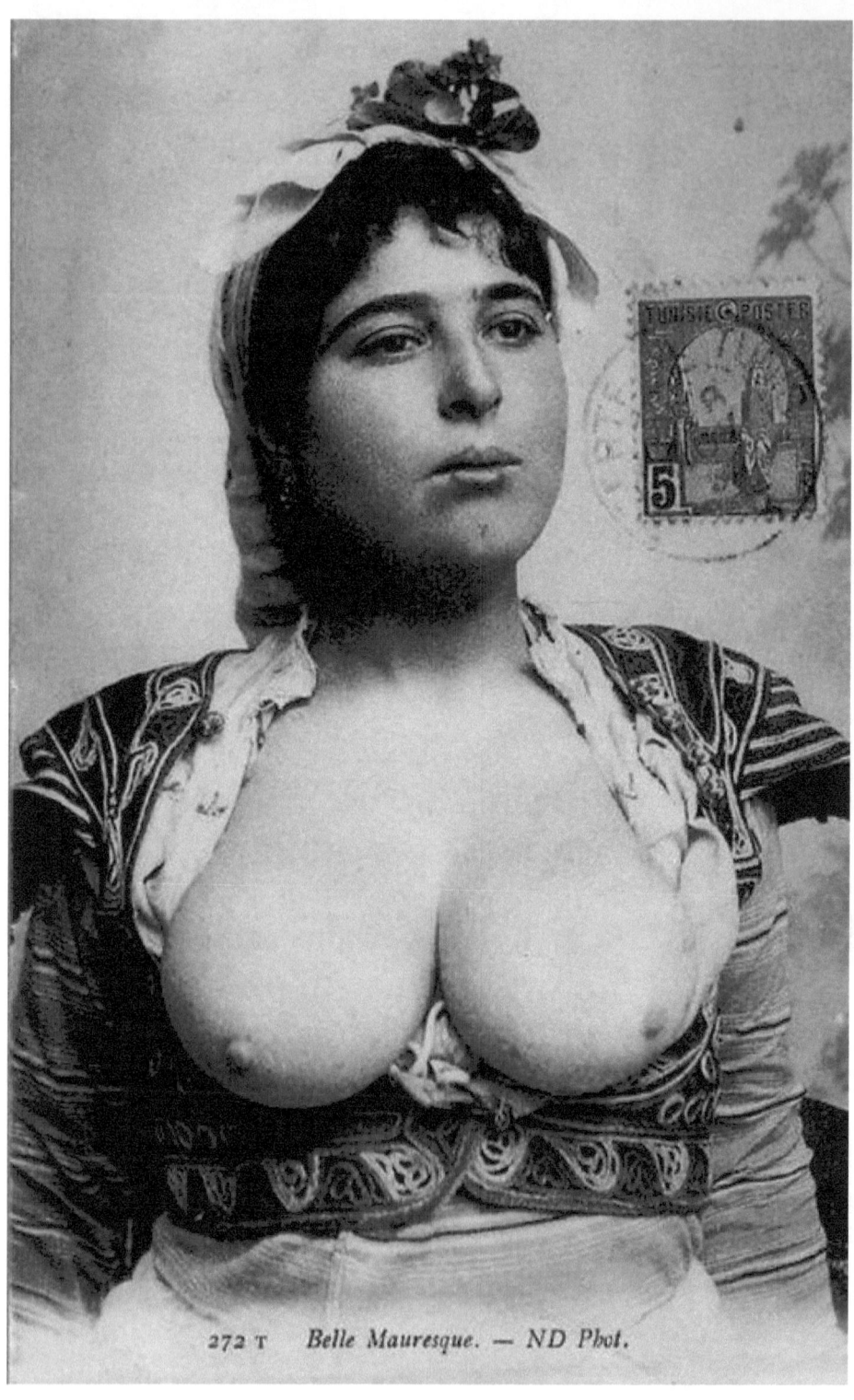

272 T Belle Mauresque. — ND Phot.

243 A — Mauresque. ND Phot.

Jeune Mauresque

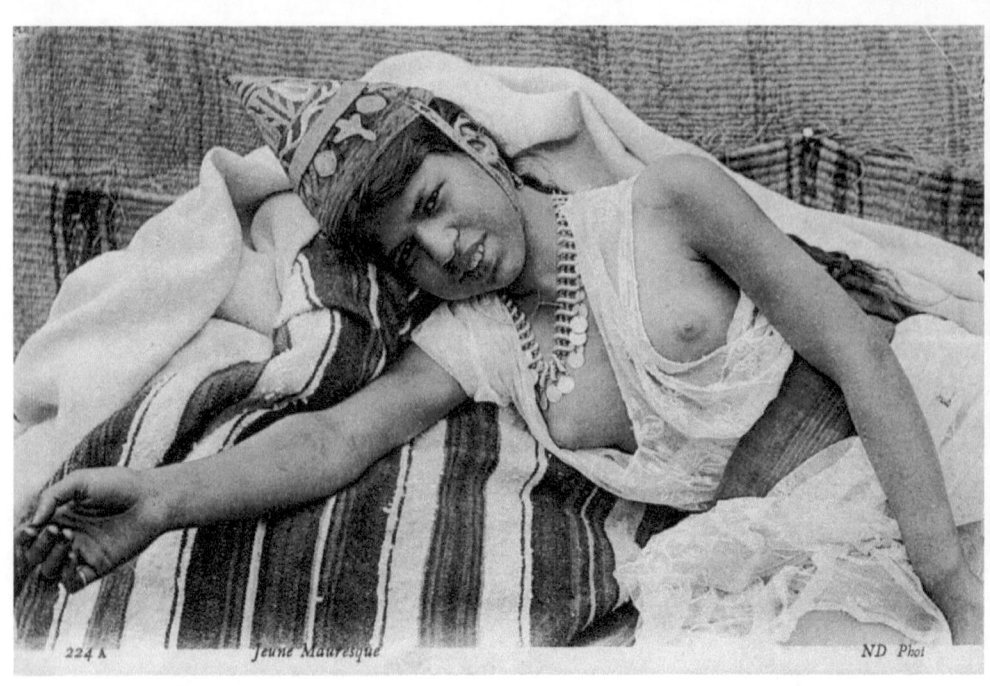

Jeune Fille Mauresque

Jeune Fille Mauresque

219 A — Jeune Fille mauresque. ND Phot.

TUNISIE. — Bédouine

Femme Kabyle se couvrant de son Haïck

Collections ND Phot

Femme Mauresque

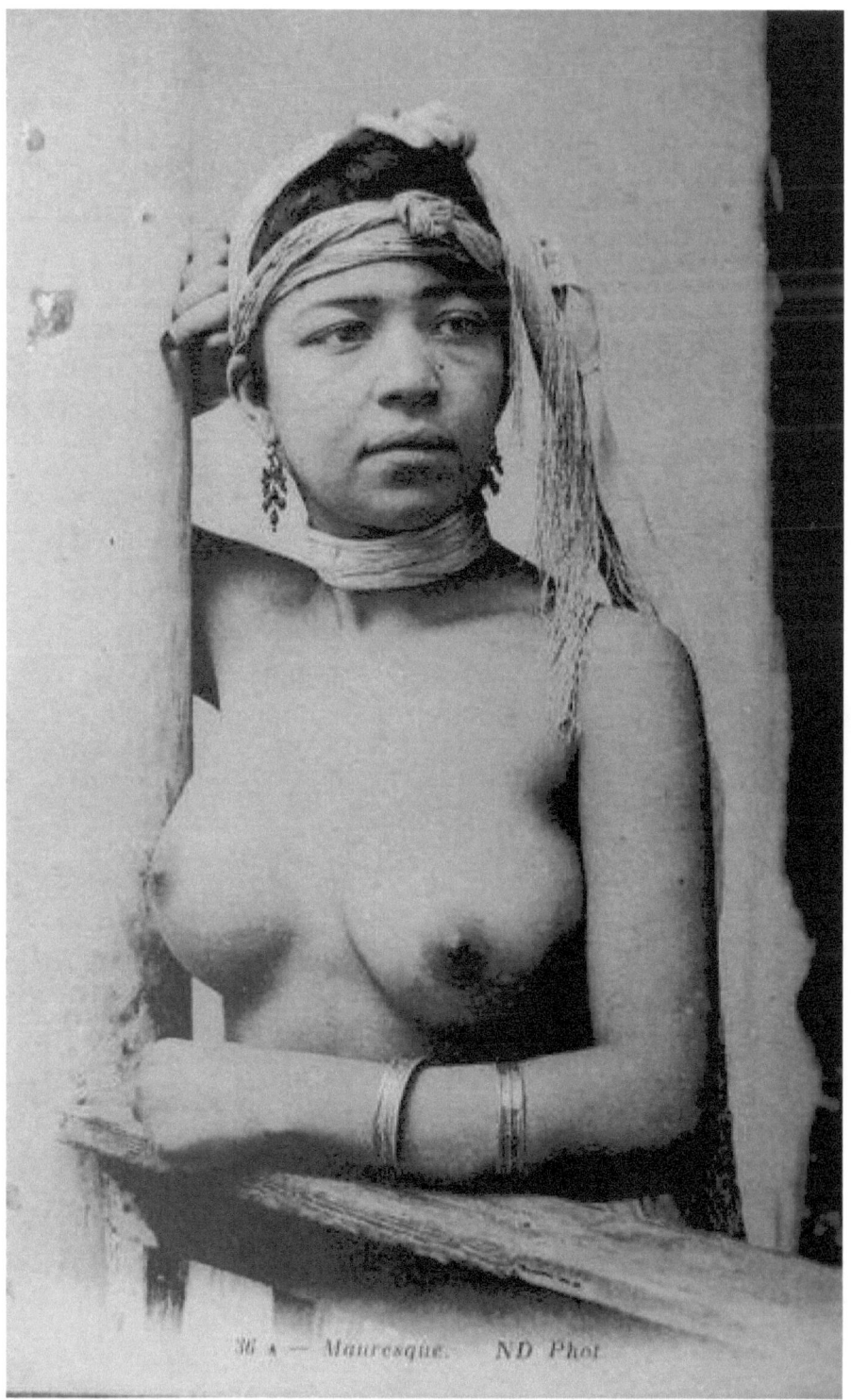

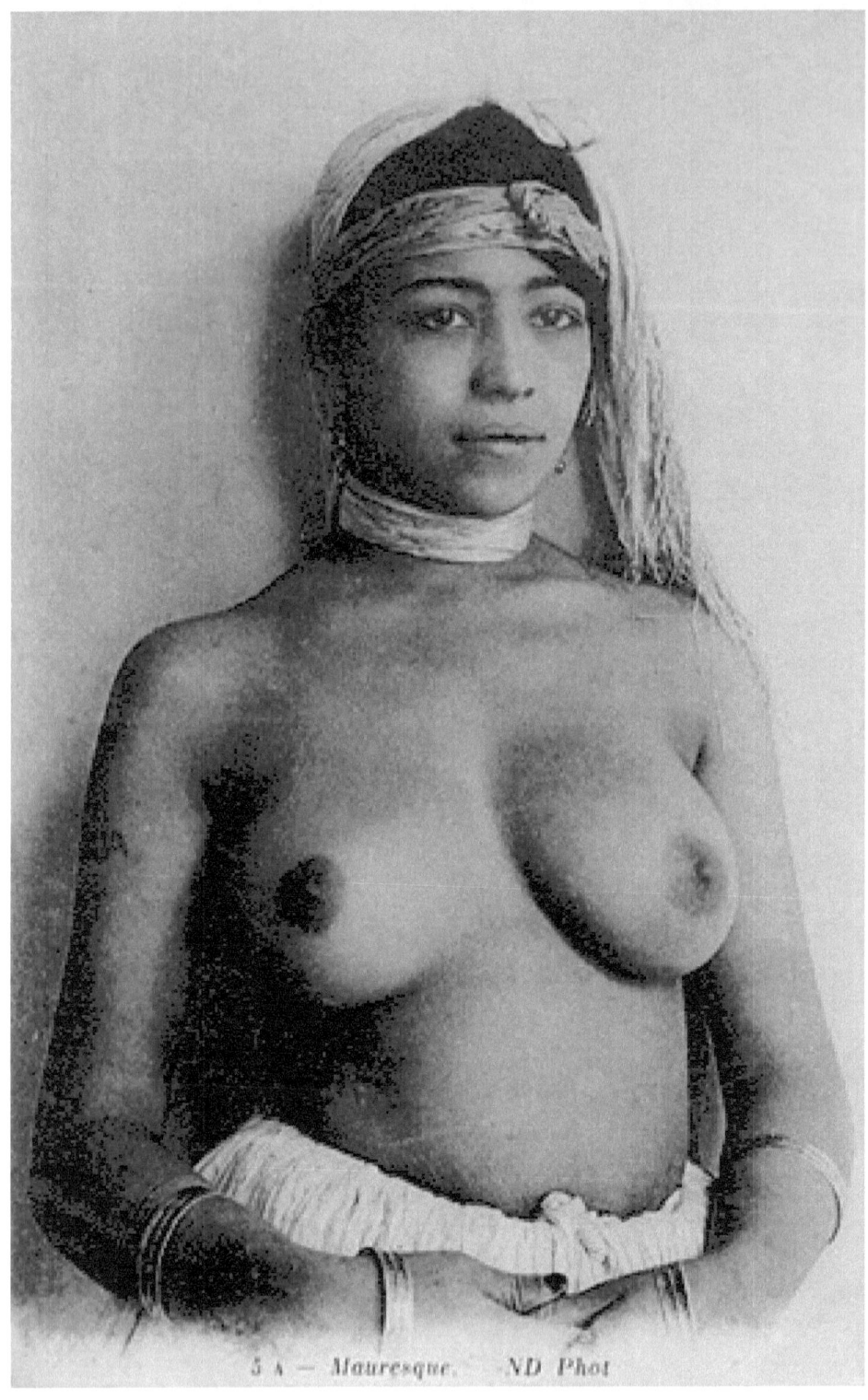

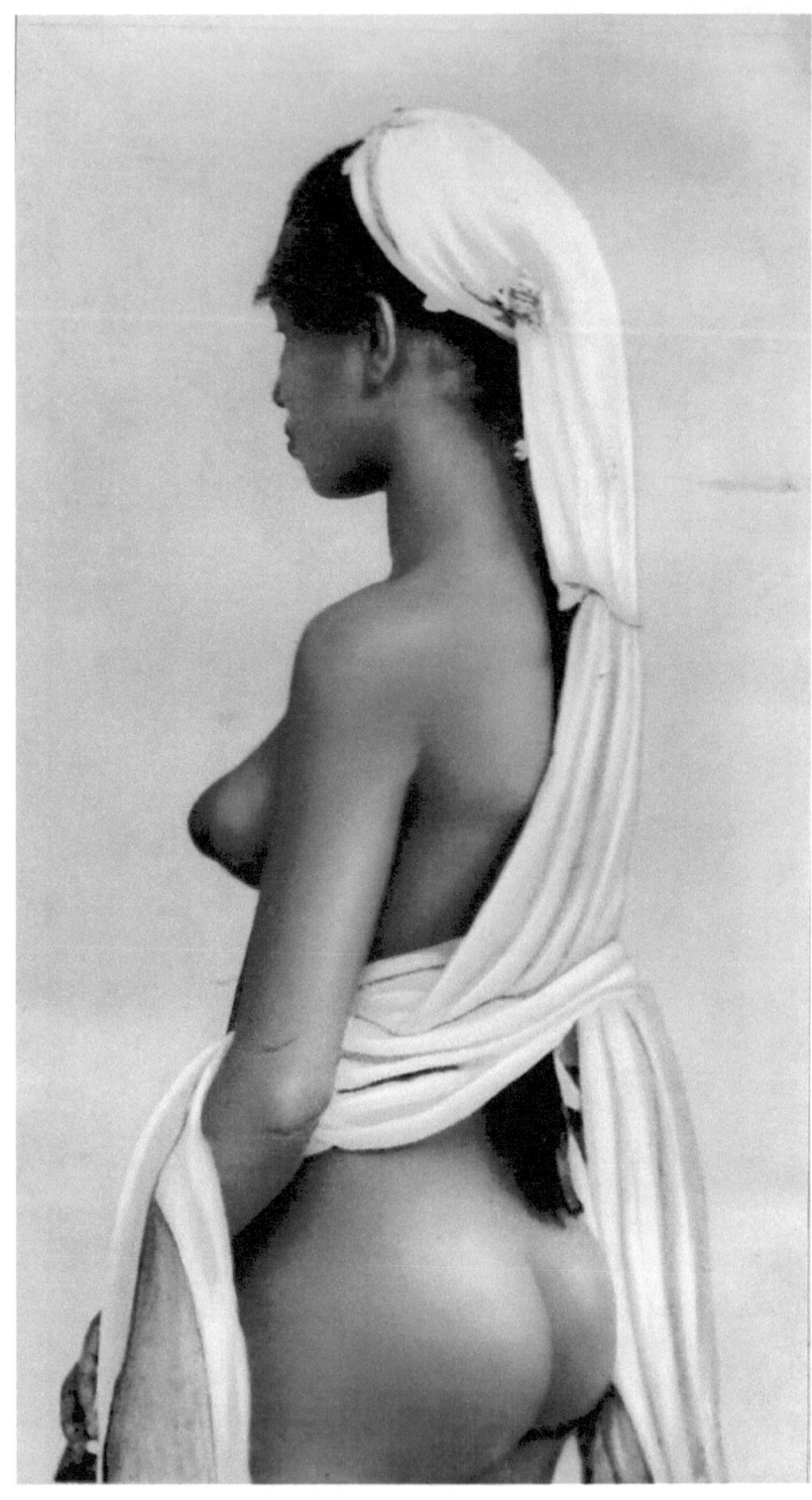

www.ingramcontent.com/pod-product-compliance
Lightning Source LLC
Chambersburg PA
CBHW030754180526
45163CB00003B/1015